Utilize este código QR para se cadastrar de forma mais rápida:

Ou, se preferir, entre em:
www.richmond.com.br/ac/livroportal
e siga as instruções para ter acesso aos conteúdos exclusivos do
Portal e Livro Digital

CÓDIGO DE ACESSO:
A 00092 TBIENGK1E 1 77748

Faça apenas um cadastro. Ele será válido para:

From trees to books,
sustainability all the way

Da semente ao livro,
sustentabilidade por todo o caminho

Planting forests
The wood used as raw material for our paper comes from planted forests, that is, it is not the result of deforestation. This practice generates thousands of jobs for farmers and helps to recover environmentally degraded areas.

Plantar florestas
A madeira que serve de matéria-prima para nosso papel vem de plantio renovável, ou seja, não é fruto de desmatamento. Essa prática gera milhares de empregos para agricultores e ajuda a recuperar áreas ambientais degradadas.

Making paper and printing books
The entire paper production chain, from pulp production to book binding, is certified, complying with international standards for sustainable processing and environmental best practices.

Fabricar papel e imprimir livros
Toda a cadeia produtiva do papel, desde a produção de celulose até a encadernação do livro, é certificada, cumprindo padrões internacionais de processamento sustentável e boas práticas ambientais.

Creating content
Our educational solutions are developed with life-long goals guided by editorial values, diverse viewpoints and socio-environmental responsibility.

Criar conteúdos
Os profissionais envolvidos na elaboração de nossas soluções educacionais buscam uma educação para a vida pautada por curadoria editorial, diversidade de olhares e responsabilidade socioambiental.

Developing life projects
Richmond educational solutions are an act of commitment to the future of younger generations, enabling partnerships between schools and families in their mission to educate!

Construir projetos de vida
Oferecer uma solução educacional Richmond é um ato de comprometimento com o futuro das novas gerações, possibilitando uma relação de parceria entre escolas e famílias na missão de educar!

Scan the QR code to learn more.
Access *https://mod.lk/rich_sus*

Fotografe o código QR e conheça melhor esse caminho.
Saiba mais em *https://mod.lk/rich_sus*

THE BIG IDEA 1
English for Kids

Editora responsável:
Izaura Valverde

Richmond

Direção editorial: Sandra Possas

Edição executiva de inglês: Izaura Valverde
Edição executiva de produção e multimídia: Adriana Pedro de Almeida

Coordenação de arte e produção: Raquel Buim
Coordenação de revisão: Rafael Spigel

Edição de texto: Giuliana Gramani, Thelma Babaoka
Elaboração de conteúdo: Adriana Saporito, Thelma Babaoka
Preparação de originais: Helaine Albuquerque
Revisão: Carolina Waideman, Flora Vaz Manzione, Gisele Ribeiro Fujii, Kandy Saraiva, Lucila Vrublevicius Segóvia, Márcia Suzumura, Márcio Martins, Marina Gomes, Vivian Cristina de Souza

Projeto gráfico: Karina de Sá
Edição de arte: Karina de Sá
Diagramação: Casa de Ideias
Capa: Fabiane Eugenio
Ilustração da capa: Carlitos Pinheiro
Ilustrações: Artur Fujita, Bianca de Aguiar Oliveira, Brenda Bossato, Bruna Assis Brasil, Carlitos Pinheiro, Chris Borges, Claudia Marianno, Claudio Chiyo, Daniel Linard, Danillo Souza, Fabiana Salomão, Gordei, Gra Mattar, Laís Bicudo, Leo Teixeira, Lucas Reis Pereira, Marcos de Mello, Marcos Llussá, Maria Rigon, Mauro Souza, Michel Ramalho, Michele Cavaloti, Pablo Zamboni, Raíssa Lima Bulhões de Luna, Raitan Ohi, Renam Penante, Ricardo Chucky, Rodrigo Cordeiro, Tintavlek, Wandson de Oliveira Rocha
Artes: Carol Duran, Manuel Miramontes, Marina Prado, Priscila Wu

Real-Time View (RTV): Gabrielle Navarro (edição de conteúdo); Amanda Miyuki, Mônica M. Oldrine (*design*); Gislaine Caprioli, Letícia Della Giacoma de França (revisão)
Portal Educacional Richmond: Gabrielle Navarro (edição e curadoria de conteúdo); Maria Eduarda Scetta (curadoria de conteúdo); Amanda Miyuki (*design*); Eloah Cristina (analista de projeto); Gislaine Caprioli, Letícia Della Giacoma de França (revisão)
Adventureland: Gabrielle Navarro (elaboração e edição de conteúdo); Daniel Favalli (produção); Mônica M. Oldrine (*design*); Gislaine Caprioli, Letícia Della Giacoma de França (revisão)
Digital Academy for Kids: Gabrielle Navarro (elaboração e edição de conteúdo); Daniel Favalli (produção); Mônica M. Oldrine (*design*); Gislaine Caprioli, Letícia Della Giacoma de França (revisão)
Livro Digital Interativo: Gabrielle Navarro (edição de conteúdo); Daniel Favalli (produção); Mônica M. Oldrine (*design*); Gislaine Caprioli, Letícia Della Giacoma de França (revisão)
Livro Digital para Projeção: Gabrielle Navarro (edição de conteúdo); Amanda Miyuki (*design*); Eloah Cristina (analista de projeto); Gislaine Caprioli, Letícia Della Giacoma de França (revisão)

Iconografia: Ellen Silvestre, Eveline Duarte, Paloma Klein, Sara Alencar
Coordenação de *bureau*: Rubens M. Rodrigues
Tratamento de imagens: Ademir Francisco Baptista, Joel Aparecido, Luiz Carlos Costa, Marina M. Buzzinaro, Vânia Aparecida M. de Oliveira
Pré-impressão: Alexandre Petreca, Everton L. de Oliveira, Fabio Roldan, Marcio H. Kamoto, Ricardo Rodrigues, Vitória Sousa
Áudio: Núcleo de Criação Produções em Áudio

Todos os *sites* mencionados nesta obra foram reproduzidos apenas para fins didáticos. A Richmond não tem controle sobre seu conteúdo, o qual foi cuidadosamente verificado antes de sua utilização.

Websites mentioned in this material were quoted for didactic purposes only. Richmond has no control over their content and urges care when using them.

Embora todas as medidas tenham sido tomadas para identificar e contatar os detentores de direitos autorais sobre os materiais reproduzidos nesta obra, isso nem sempre foi possível. A editora estará pronta a retificar quaisquer erros dessa natureza assim que notificada.

Every effort has been made to trace the copyright holders, but if any omission can be rectified, the publishers will be pleased to make the necessary arrangements.

Impressão e acabamento: HRosa Gráfica e Editora
Lote: 797804 **Cod:** 120002130

Dados Internacionais de Catalogação na Publicação (CIP)
(Câmara Brasileira do Livro, SP, Brasil)

The big idea : English for kids / obra coletiva concebida, organizada, desenvolvida e produzida pela Editora Moderna ; editora responsável Izaura Valverde. -- 1. ed. -- São Paulo : Moderna, 2021.

Obra em 5 v. para alunos do 1º ao 5º ano.

1. Inglês (Ensino fundamental) I. Valverde, Izaura.

21-65926 CDD-372.652

Índices para catálogo sistemático:
1. Inglês : Ensino fundamental 372.652
Cibele Maria Dias - Bibliotecária - CRB-8/9427

ISBN 978-65-5779-836-2 (LA)
ISBN 978-65-5779-837-9 (LP)

Reprodução proibida. Art. 184 do Código Penal e Lei 9.610 de 19 de fevereiro de 1998.

Todos os direitos reservados.

RICHMOND
SANTILLANA EDUCAÇÃO LTDA.
Rua Padre Adelino, 758, 3º andar – Belenzinho
São Paulo – SP – Brasil – CEP 03303-904
www.richmond.com.br
2024

Impresso no Brasil

CÓPIA NÃO AUTORIZADA É CRIME
ABDR
ASSOCIAÇÃO BRASILEIRA DE DIREITOS REPROGRÁFICOS
RESPEITE O DIREITO AUTORAL

Créditos das fotos: p. 10: pixdeluxe/iStockphoto, Georgijevic/iStockphoto; p. 11: JudyKennamer/iStockphoto, laflor/iStockphoto, shapecharge/iStockphoto, PeopleImages/iStockphoto, bowdenimages/iStockphoto, kali9/iStockphoto, FatCamera/iStockphoto, kali9/iStockphoto, NADOFOTOS/iStockphoto, jpmediainc/iStockphoto, PeopleImages/iStockphoto, Poike/iStockphoto; p. 12: Fernando Favoretto; p. 14: monkeybusinessimages/iStockphoto, monkeybusinessimages/iStockphoto, monkeybusinessimages/iStockphoto, Lisitsa/iStockphoto, miharayou/iStockphoto; p. 15: ljubaphoto/iStockphoto, monkeybusinessimages/iStockphoto; p. 18: zak00/iStockphoto, klyaksun/iStockphoto; p. 19: precinbe/iStockphoto; p. 20: Fernando Favoretto, filkjusto/Shutterstock; p. 21: klyaksun/iStockphoto; p. 22: Tashi-Delek/iStockphoto, PeterHermesFurian/iStockphoto; p. 23: Private Collection, Städtische Galerie im Lenbachhaus, Munich; p 24: Olga Kurbatova/iStockphoto, thedafkish/iStockphoto; p. 25: zhaojiankang/iStockphoto, PeterHermesFurian/iStockphoto; p. 28: Lucia Kindernayova/iStockphoto, Capuski/iStockphoto, Evgeniia Iakimenko/iStockphoto, gyro/iStockphoto, Brina Bunt/iStockphoto, sergeyryzhov/iStockphoto; p. 29: Panya_sealim/iStockphoto, Tetiana Garkusha/iStockphoto, Freer Law/iStockphoto, sergeyryzhov/iStockphoto; p. 30: Fernando Favoretto; p. 31: Julia Lazebnaya/iStockphoto, PCH-Vector/iStockphoto, Sudowoodo/iStockphoto; p. 32: Harald Schmidt/iStockphoto, Young777/iStockphoto, 4FR/iStockphoto, FurmanAnna/iStockphoto, Narongrit Sritana/iStockphoto, shellhawker/iStockphoto; p. 33: Sasiistock/iStockphoto, CasarsaGuru/iStockphoto, andresr/iStockphoto, Mordolff/iStockphoto; p. 36: olga_sweet/iStockphoto; p. 37: Lisitsa/iStockphoto, DDurrich/iStockphoto, Lisa5201/iStockphoto, ozgurcankaya/iStockphoto, HRAUN/iStockphoto, salez/iStockphoto, Meranna/iStockphoto, PK-Photos/iStockphoto, Ivailo Nikolov/Shutterstock, 35007/iStockphoto, alexsich/iStockphoto; p. 38: Fernando Favoretto; p. 39: Igor Zakowski/iStockphoto; p. 41: RapidEye/iStockphoto, Sasiistock/iStockphoto, Berezko/iStockphoto, VladimirFLoyd/iStockphoto; p. 42: Imgorthand/iStockphoto, DjelicS/iStockphoto; p. 43: ONYXprj/iStockphoto, FatCamera/iStockphoto, izusek/iStockphoto, LumineImages/iStockphoto, m-imagephotography/iStockphoto; p. 46: Friday Night/Shutterstock, malerapaso/iStockphoto, Galina Tolochko/iStockphoto, ThomasVogel/iStockphoto, Lis Faino/iStockphoto, benemaleistock/iStockphoto, avtk/iStockphoto, sapto7/iStockphoto; p. 48: blackCAT/iStockphoto, Patrick_BOUDINET/iStockphoto, jordieasy/iStockphoto, Shelly Still/Shutterstock, Camellia Vintage/iStockphoto, Eshma/iStockphoto, Lazartivan/iStockphoto, Armelle LLobet/iStockphoto; p. 50: atakan/iStockphoto, gbrundin/iStockphoto, gldburger/iStockphoto, photka/iStockphoto, canbedone/Shutterstock, matmart/iStockphoto, Chunhai Cao/iStockphoto, Yobro10/iStockphoto, Tomacco/iStockphoto; p. 51: SerrNovik/iStockphoto, katleho Seisa/iStockphoto, SDI Productions/iStockphoto; p. 54: Sasiistock/iStockphoto, TShum/iStockphoto, lucielang/iStockphoto, Supersmario/iStockphoto, bonetta/iStockphoto, 17rst/iStockphoto, 17rst/iStockphoto; p. 55: FatCamera/iStockphoto, martin-dm/iStockphoto, paulaphoto/iStockphoto, Strekalova/iStockphoto, Littlewitz/iStockphoto, VectorHot/iStockphoto, S-S-S/iStockphoto, S-S-S/iStockphoto; p. 56: Fernando Favoretto; p. 57: eliflamra/iStockphoto; p. 58: Dotta 2; p. 60: venusphoto/iStockphoto, Niall_Majury/iStockphoto, FotoDuets/iStockphoto, JazzIRT/iStockphoto, calvindexter/iStockphoto, ONYXprj/iStockphoto; p. 64: PC Photography/iStockphoto, KatarzynaBialasiewicz/iStockphoto, Korakoch Sookkerd/iStockphoto, LeslieLauren/iStockphoto, onurdongel/iStockphoto, Elenathewise/iStockphoto; p. 65: aodaodaod/iStockphoto, baona/iStockphoto, justhavealook/iStockphoto, Mariia Demchenko/iStockphoto, onurdongel/iStockphoto, contrastaddict/iStockphoto, KatarzynaBialasiewicz/iStockphoto, poligonchik/iStockphoto, Brankospejs/iStockphoto, contrastaddict/iStockphoto; p. 66: LeManna/iStockphoto, Macrovector/iStockphoto; p. 67: Mykhailo Ridkous/iStockphoto, ArdeaA/iStockphoto; p. 68: irina88w/iStockphoto, wuttichaijangrab/iStockphoto, Edita Meskoniene/iStockphoto, Intergalactic Rada/iStockphoto; p. 72: sabyna75/iStockphoto, ValentynVolkov/iStockphoto, Mariha-kitchen/iStockphoto, Zakharova_Natalia/iStockphoto, naturalbox/iStockphoto, Alter_photo/iStockphoto, Prostock-Studio/iStockphoto; p. 73: bergamont/iStockphoto, TeamDAF/iStockphoto, MediaProduction/iStockphoto, the-lightwriter/iStockphoto, bluestocking/iStockphoto, JoeGough/iStockphoto, ClaudioVentrella/iStockphoto; p. 74: DNF-Style/iStockphoto, Jelena Zikic/iStockphoto, wideonet/iStockphoto, bhofack2/iStockphoto, pilipphoto/iStockphoto, artisteer/iStockphoto, cagkansayin/iStockphoto, DebbiSmirnoff/iStockphoto, arthobbit/iStockphoto; p. 76: ArtMarie/iStockphoto, RichLegg/iStockphoto, Johnny Greig/iStockphoto, Imgorthand/iStockphoto, FatCamera/iStockphoto, Nuttawut_phet/iStockphoto, DianaHirsch/iStockphoto, SasaJo/iStockphoto, chanuth/iStockphoto, Hyrma/iStockphoto, Lipe Borges/iStockphoto, gustavomellossa/iStockphoto; p. 77: max-kegfire/iStockphoto, karelnoppe/iStockphoto, skynesher/iStockphoto, lyulka/iStockphoto, pijama61/iStockphoto, RENGraphic/iStockphoto; p. 78: chuckcollier/iStockphoto, KatarzynaBialasiewicz/iStockphoto, elenaleonova/iStockphoto, TerryJ/iStockphoto; p. 80: BiancaGrueneberg/iStockphoto, ilona75/iStockphoto, studiohoto/iStockphoto; p. 81: Ksenia Zvezdina/iStockphoto, diane555/iStockphoto, Kuzmichstudio/iStockphoto, Itsadream/Dreamstime/Glow Images, bpperry/iStockphoto, Mawardibahar/iStockphoto, Fernando Favoretto/Criar Imagem, Dotta2; p. 85: FatCamera/iStockphoto, arinahabich/iStockphoto, Rita Szilvasi/Shutterstock, heidijpix/iStockphoto, virtustudio/iStockphoto; p. 86: aetb/iStockphoto, Pekic/iStockphoto, pixelfusion3d/iStockphoto, hkeita/iStockphoto, Alena Igdeeva/iStockphoto; p. 87: lithiumcloud/iStockphoto, LumenSt/iStockphoto, Mirjana Ristic/iStockphoto, filipefrazao/iStockphoto, FerreiraSilva/iStockphoto; p. 88: YinYang/iStockphoto, kertlis/iStockphoto, yotrak/iStockphoto; p. 89: galbiati/iStockphoto; p. 90: gpointstudio/iStockphoto, monkeybusinessimages/iStockphoto; p. 91: ksana-gribakina/iStockphoto; p. 92: Bilanol/iStockphoto, FangXiaNuo/iStockphoto, amoklv/iStockphoto, traveler1116/iStockphoto, Konoplytska/iStockphoto, benedek/iStockphoto, Private Collection, Musée National d'Art Moderne/Centre de création industrielle/Centre Pompidou/Paris, Museum of Modern Art, New York, Nenov/iStockphoto, Satakorn/iStockphoto, cenkertekin/iStockphoto, Lucia Gajdosikova/iStockphoto; p. 93: Sharlotta/iStockphoto, Лилия Альбертовна Галеева/iStockphoto, ayutaka/iStockphoto, ayutaka/iStockphoto, Lili Kudrili/Shutterstock, Irina_Strelnikova/iStockphoto; p. 94: pkphotoscom/iStockphoto, Vladyslav Danilin/iStockphoto, italiansight/iStockphoto, Lepro/iStockphoto, MashaStarus/iStockphoto; p. 97: Chunhai Cao/iStockphoto, Picsfive/iStockphoto, dandanian/iStockphoto, bdspn/iStockphoto, offstocker/iStockphoto, ilterriorm/iStockphoto, Iaroslav Bushuev/iStockphoto, Colorfuel Studio/iStockphoto; p. 98: yipengge/iStockphoto, Тодорчук Екатерина/iStockphoto, Balakleypb/iStockphoto, obeyleesin/iStockphoto, luckyraccoon/iStockphoto, kieferpix/iStockphoto, no107/iStockphoto, ozgurcankaya/iStockphoto, valio84sl/iStockphoto, Lemon_tm/iStockphoto, Chillim/iStockphoto, nomadphotography/iStockphoto; p. 99: Bigmouse108/iStockphoto; p. 100: Tina_Rencelj/iStockphoto, Pogonici/iStockphoto, mihalec/iStockphoto, kyoshino/iStockphoto, goir/iStockphoto, esseffe/iStockphoto, drpnncpp/iStockphoto, design56/iStockphoto; p. 101: KatarzynaBialasiewicz/iStockphoto, Alexey Shipilov/iStockphoto, imaginima/iStockphoto, Buffy1982/iStockphoto; p. 102: doodlemachine/iStockphoto, KatarzynaBialasiewicz/iStockphoto, DoraDalton/iStockphoto, CreativaStudio/iStockphoto, CreativaStudio/iStockphoto, JoeGough/iStockphoto, Onzeg/iStockphoto; p. 103: Anna_zabella/iStockphoto, Jane_Kelly/iStockphoto, ikuvshinov/iStockphoto, Feodora Chiosea/iStockphoto; p. 104: Vasyl Faievych/iStockphoto, 4nadia/iStockphoto, Brycia James/iStockphoto, ugurv/iStockphoto, olvas/iStockphoto, Xesai/iStockphoto, bhofack2/iStockphoto, Chatri Attanatwong/iStockphoto; p. 105: Marina/iStockphoto; p. 113: krailurk/iStockphoto, venusphoto/iStockphoto, AlexLMX/iStockphoto, CTRPhotos/iStockphoto, zayatssv/iStockphoto, bdspn/iStockphoto, camaralenta/iStockphoto; p. 115: Sky_Blue/iStockphoto, Mega Pixel/Shutterstock, LumenSt/iStockphoto, Garsya/iStockphoto, dlerick/iStockphoto, Witthaya/iStockphoto, Mordolff/iStockphoto; p. 119: organi/iStockphoto, Odu Mazza/iStockphoto, ibeirorocha/iStockphoto, ligora/iStockphoto, ligora/iStockphoto, artisteer/iStockphoto, SasaJo/iStockphoto.

CONTENTS

SCOPE AND SEQUENCE 4
WELCOME 6

UNIT 1
MY FAMILY 8
HERE AND NOW 15

UNIT 2
FUN WITH COLORS 16
CLIL 23   REVIEW 1 & 2 24

UNIT 3
ALL ABOUT PETS 26
HERE AND NOW 33

UNIT 4
THIS IS MY BODY 34
CLIL 41   REVIEW 3 & 4 42

UNIT 5
LET'S PLAY! 44
HERE AND NOW 51

UNIT 6
IT'S TIME TO STUDY 52
CLIL 59   REVIEW 5 & 6 60

UNIT 7
THIS IS MY HOME! 62
HERE AND NOW 69

UNIT 8
LET'S HAVE A PICNIC! 70
CLIL 77   REVIEW 7 & 8 78

HANDS ON 80
GAME 82
INSTRUCTIONS 84
GLOSSARY 85
WORKBOOK 89
PRESS-OUTS 105
STICKERS 121

SCOPE AND SEQUENCE

Unidade	Objetivos	Conteúdo linguístico	Conteúdo digital	CLIL / Here and Now	Apêndices
Welcome – p. 6					
1 **My Family** p. 8	▶ Apresentar os membros da família. ▶ Descrever se uma família é pequena ou grande. ▶ Refletir sobre a importância do respeito aos idosos.	*brother, dad, grandma, grandpa, mom, sister; big family, small family* *This is my (brother). / Oh, and this is me! / I love my family!*	GIF: família	**Here and Now:** Respeito aos idosos.	**Workbook** p. 89
2 **Fun with Colors** p. 16	▶ Falar sobre os brinquedos de um *playground*. ▶ Descrever as cores dos brinquedos de um *playground*. ▶ Perguntar sobre a cor favorita de alguém e dizer qual é sua cor favorita. ▶ Refletir sobre cores em obras de arte.	*ball pit, jungle gym, seesaw, slide, swing, trampoline; black, blue, brown, gray, green, orange, pink, purple, red, white, yellow* *What color is it? It's (blue). / The (slide) is (orange). / What's your favorite color? My favorite color is (green).*	Quiz: cores	**CLIL: Arte** – Cores.	**Workbook** p. 91
Review 1 & 2 – p. 24					
3 **All about Pets** p. 26	▶ Perguntar e responder sobre animais de estimação. ▶ Perguntar e responder sobre quantidades de animais de estimação. ▶ Refletir sobre o que podemos aprender com animais de estimação.	*cat, dog, ferret, hamster, rabbit, turtle; numbers 1-10* *What's this? It's a (turtle). It's cute. / How many (dogs)? (Three.)*	Infográfico: animais de estimação	**Here and Now:** *Mindfulness* com animais de estimação.	**Workbook** p. 93 **Hands on** p. 80
4 **This is My Body** p. 34	▶ Falar sobre as partes do corpo e suas quantidades. ▶ Reconhecer as funções das partes do corpo. ▶ Empregar comandos simples relacionados à utilização das partes do corpo em uma dança. ▶ Refletir sobre higiene e limpeza do corpo.	*arms, ears, eyes, feet, hands, head, legs, mouth, nose* *I have (one mouth) and (two legs). / Clap your hands! / Move your arms! / Stamp your feet! / Touch your head!*	Infográfico: corpo humano	**CLIL: Ciências** – O corpo humano.	**Workbook** p. 95
Review 3 & 4 – p. 42					

Unidade	Objetivos	Conteúdo linguístico	Conteúdo digital	CLIL / Here and Now	Apêndices
5 Let's Play! p. 44	▶ Falar sobre brinquedos. ▶ Perguntar sobre o brinquedo favorito de alguém e dizer qual é o próprio brinquedo favorito. ▶ Refletir sobre a importância da iniciativa e da cooperação.	*an art set, a ball, a bike, a car, a doll, a kite, a teddy bear* *What's this? It's (a ball/an art set). / What's your favorite toy? My favorite toy is (a kite).*	Jogo da memória: brinquedos	**Here and Now:** Cooperação.	**Workbook** p. 97 **Hands on** p. 81
6 It's Time to Study p. 52	▶ Falar sobre materiais escolares e descrever suas cores. ▶ Pedir emprestados e emprestar materiais escolares. ▶ Refletir sobre o uso consciente de materiais e o descarte adequado de lixo.	*a backpack, a book, a crayon, an eraser, a notebook, a pen, a pencil* *I need (an eraser), please. Here you are. Thank you.*	GIF: materiais escolares	**CLIL: Ciências** – Objetos escolares.	**Workbook** p. 99
Review 5 & 6 – p. 60					
7 This is My Home! p. 62	▶ Nomear as diferentes partes da casa. ▶ Reconhecer formas geométricas em elementos encontrados em um ambiente. ▶ Falar sobre a localização de pessoas e objetos na casa. ▶ Refletir sobre a importância do *mindfulness* para a organização.	*bathroom, bedroom, dining room, kitchen, living room, yard; circle, rectangle, square, triangle* *Where's (Mom)? In the living room. / Look, a (square)!*	Vídeo: *Hide and seek*	**Here and Now:** Usando *mindfulness* na organização.	**Workbook** p. 101
8 Let's Have a Picnic! p. 70	▶ Falar sobre alimentos que podem ser consumidos em um piquenique. ▶ Dizer de quais alimentos gosta e de quais não gosta. ▶ Perguntar a opinião de outras pessoas sobre os alimentos. ▶ Refletir sobre alimentação e vestuário em relação às condições climáticas.	*apples, bananas, cake, cookies, milk, orange juice, toast; I don't like, I like, I love* *I (don't) like/love (milk). And you? I (don't) like/love (orange juice).*	Jogo de tabuleiro: piquenique	**CLIL: Geografia** – Alimentação e vestuário.	**Workbook** p. 103
Review 7 & 8 – p. 78					

Game – p. 82   **Instructions** – p. 84   **Glossary** – p. 85   **Press-outs** – p. 105   **Stickers** – p. 121

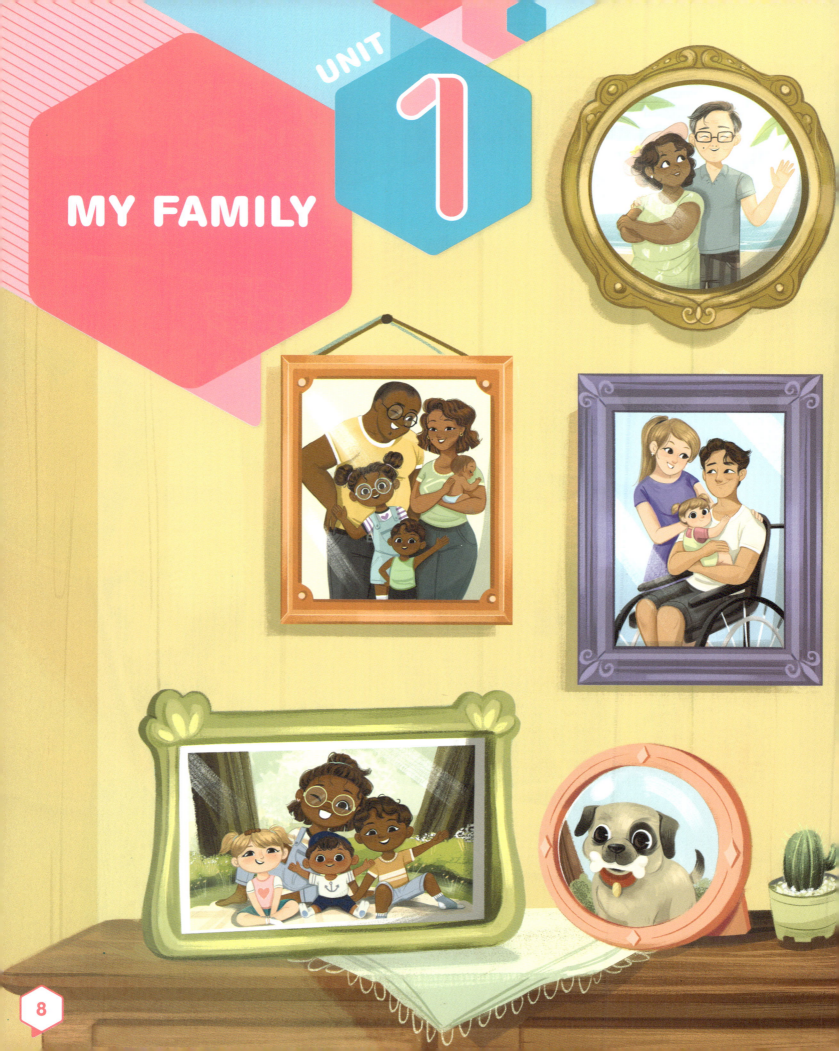

3 LOOK, LISTEN AND SAY.

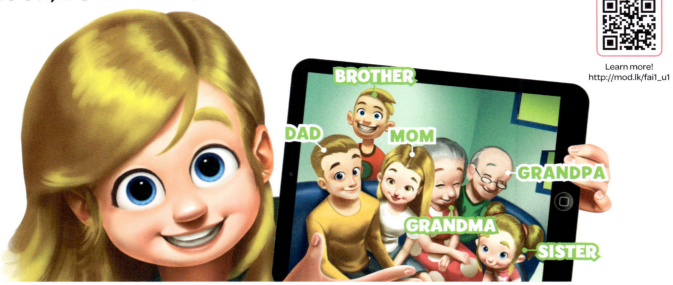

4 LOOK AND MATCH. THEN LISTEN AND CHECK.

A **BIG** FAMILY

A SMALL FAMILY

5 LISTEN, FIND AND POINT. THEN STICK.

6 LISTEN AND CHECK.

7 LISTEN AND NUMBER.

UNIT 1

8 LOOK, LISTEN AND SAY.

9 DRAW, COLOR AND TALK.

10 PRESS OUT AND TALK.

11 LISTEN AND POINT. THEN SING AND DANCE!

BIG OR SMALL?

BIG OR SMALL? BIG OR SMALL?

MY MOM AND MY DAD,
ME AND NED.
SMALL, SMALL!

BIG OR SMALL?
BIG OR SMALL?

MY MOM AND MY DAD,
MY BABY BROTHER
AND MY SISTER,
MY GRANDMA AND MY GRANDPA.
OH, AND TED.
BIG, BIG!

BIG OR SMALL? BIG OR SMALL?
IT DOESN'T MATTER,
JUST LOVE THEM ALL!

UNIT 1

12 LOOK, LISTEN AND NUMBER.

A □
B □
C 1

13 PLAY TIC-TAC-TOE.

RESPECT THE ELDERLY

1. LOOK, THINK AND CHECK.

2. LOOK, THINK AND DRAW.

UNIT 2

3 LOOK, LISTEN AND SAY.

1. BALL PIT
2. JUNGLE GYM
3. SEESAW
4. SLIDE
5. SWING
6. TRAMPOLINE

4 LOOK, LISTEN AND SAY.

BLUE   GREEN   ORANGE   PINK   PURPLE   RED   YELLOW

5 LISTEN, FIND AND NUMBER.

6 LISTEN AND CIRCLE. THEN COLOR.

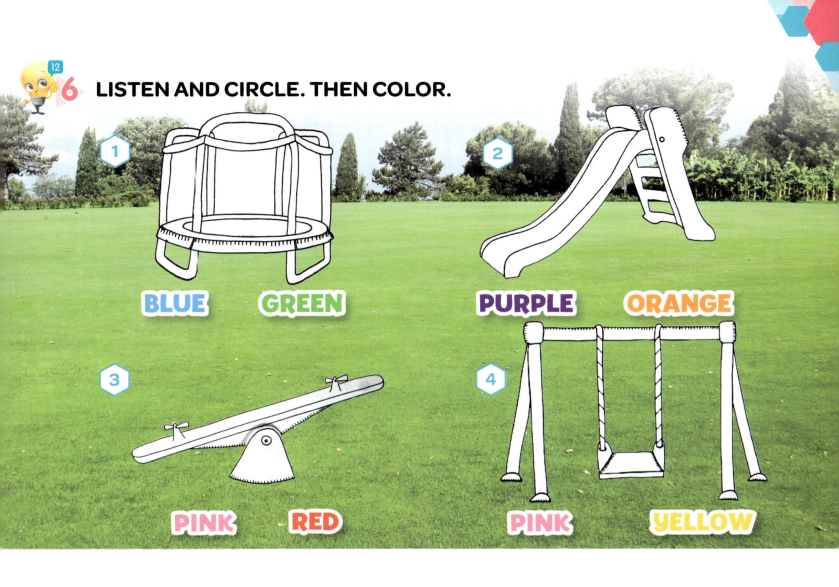

7 LOOK, THINK AND STICK.

8 **LOOK, LISTEN AND SAY.**

9 **COLOR AND TALK.**

10 LISTEN, SING AND PLAY!

PLAYGROUND FUN

WHAT CAN I MAKE? WHAT CAN I MAKE?

MAKE A BLUE SLIDE AND PLAY
MAKE A YELLOW SWING AND PLAY
MAKE A RED JUNGLE GYM AND PLAY

WHAT CAN I MAKE? WHAT CAN I MAKE?

MAKE A GREEN BALL PIT AND PLAY
MAKE A PINK SEESAW AND PLAY
MAKE A PURPLE TRAMPOLINE AND PLAY

WHAT CAN I MAKE? WHAT CAN I MAKE?

UNIT 2

11 LOOK, LISTEN AND SAY.

WHAT'S YOUR FAVORITE COLOR?

MY FAVORITE COLOR IS BLUE.

12 WHAT'S YOUR FAVORITE COLOR? CHECK.

13 PRESS OUT, PLAY AND TALK.

CLIL   COLORS (ART)

1 LOOK, LISTEN AND POINT.

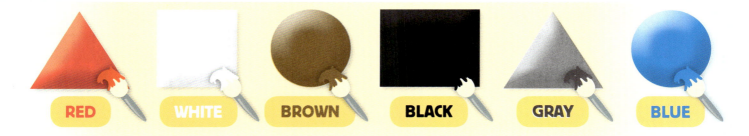

RED WHITE BROWN BLACK GRAY BLUE

2 LOOK, THINK AND SAY.

CONTRASTING SOUNDS, 1924. WASSILY KANDINSKY.

COUPLE RIDING, 1906. WASSILY KANDINSKY.

3 THINK AND DRAW.

REVIEW 1 & 2

1 LOOK, FIND AND NUMBER. THEN SAY.

2 THINK AND CIRCLE.

3 LOOK, LISTEN AND COLOR.

4 LOOK, THINK AND STICK.

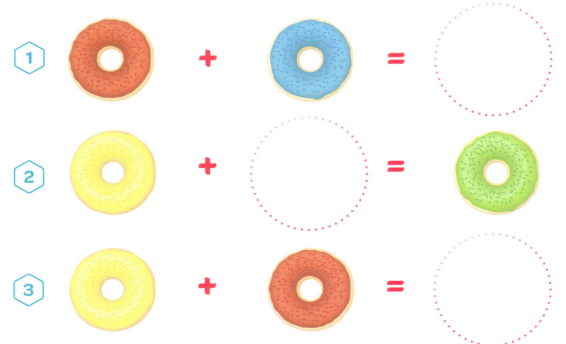

UNIT 3

 3 LOOK, LISTEN AND SAY.

1. CAT
2. DOG
3. FERRET
4. HAMSTER
5. RABBIT
6. TURTLE

4 LOOK, LISTEN AND SAY. THEN COUNT AND WRITE.

1 ONE 2 TWO 3 THREE 4 FOUR 5 FIVE 6 SIX 7 SEVEN 8 EIGHT 9 NINE 10 TEN

 A
 B
 C
 D
 E
 F

 5 LISTEN, FIND AND CIRCLE.

6 LOOK, COUNT AND CIRCLE.

A	B	C	D	E	F
3 4	3 2	5 1	4 2	6 8	7 5

7 LOOK, LISTEN AND NUMBER.

8 **LOOK, LISTEN AND SAY.**

9 **DRAW AND TALK.**

10 **PRESS OUT AND TALK.**

11 LISTEN AND STICK. THEN SING!

LITTLE PETS TO ADOPT

ONE LITTLE, TWO LITTLE, THREE LITTLE FERRETS
FOUR LITTLE, FIVE LITTLE, SIX LITTLE FERRETS
SEVEN LITTLE, EIGHT LITTLE, NINE LITTLE FERRETS
TEN LITTLE FERRETS TO ADOPT

ONE LITTLE, TWO LITTLE, THREE LITTLE CATS
FOUR LITTLE, FIVE LITTLE, SIX LITTLE CATS
SEVEN LITTLE, EIGHT LITTLE, NINE LITTLE CATS
TEN LITTLE CATS TO ADOPT

ONE LITTLE, TWO LITTLE, THREE LITTLE DOGS
FOUR LITTLE, FIVE LITTLE, SIX LITTLE DOGS
SEVEN LITTLE, EIGHT LITTLE, NINE LITTLE DOGS
TEN LITTLE DOGS TO ADOPT

12 LOOK AND MATCH. THEN COUNT AND ANSWER.

HOW MANY?

13 DRAW AND DO A PICTURE DICTATION.

32

MINDFULNESS WITH PETS

1 LOOK, LISTEN AND POINT. THEN TALK.

2 THINK AND ORDER. THEN COLOR AND TALK.

33

1 LOOK AND SAY.

2 THINK AND TALK.

35

3 LOOK, LISTEN AND SAY.

HANDS HEAD ARMS EYES NOSE EARS MOUTH LEGS FEET

Learn more!
http://mod.lk/fai1_u4

4 LISTEN AND CHECK.

 1 ☐

 2 ☐

 3 ☐

 4 ☐

5 LISTEN, FIND AND POINT.

6 LISTEN AND NUMBER.

7 LOOK, THINK AND MATCH.

8 LOOK, LISTEN AND SAY.

I HAVE THREE EYES AND ONE MOUTH.

I HAVE ONE NOSE AND FOUR FEET.

9 DRAW, COLOR AND ROLE-PLAY.

10 LISTEN, SING AND DANCE!

DANCE LIKE A ROBOT

TOUCH YOUR HEAD
LIKE A ROBOT
MOVE YOUR ARMS
LIKE A ROBOT
STAMP YOUR FEET
LIKE A ROBOT
CLAP YOUR HANDS
LIKE A ROBOT
DANCE LIKE A ROBOT

I LIKE TO TOUCH MY HEAD
LIKE A ROBOT
I LIKE TO MOVE MY ARMS
LIKE A ROBOT
I LIKE TO STAMP MY FEET
LIKE A ROBOT
I LIKE TO CLAP MY HANDS
LIKE A ROBOT
I LIKE TO DANCE
LIKE A ROBOT

11 CHOOSE AND STICK.

12 NOW DANCE!

13 PRESS OUT AND PLAY.

THE HUMAN BODY (SCIENCE)

1 LOOK AND MATCH. THEN TALK.

2 LOOK, THINK AND DRAW.

41

REVIEW 3 & 4

1   LOOK, STICK AND SAY.

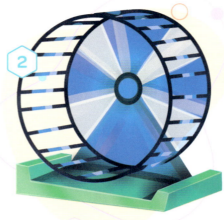

2   LISTEN AND COLOR.

3 LOOK, LISTEN AND NUMBER.

4 LOOK AND SAY. THEN PLAY SIMON SAYS.

UNIT 5

3 **LOOK, LISTEN AND SAY.**

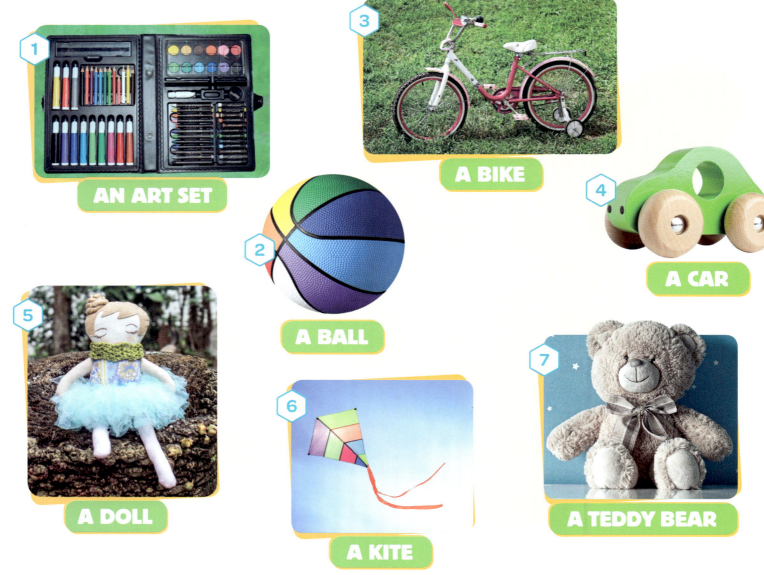

1. AN ART SET
2. A BALL
3. A BIKE
4. A CAR
5. A DOLL
6. A KITE
7. A TEDDY BEAR

4 **LISTEN AND COLOR.**

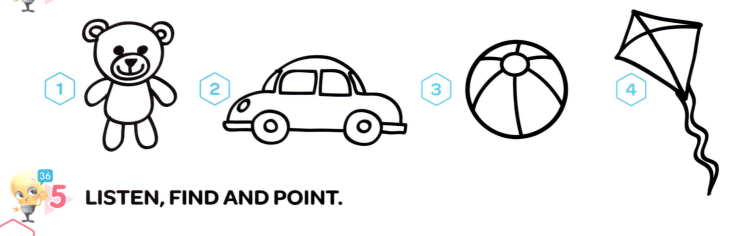

5 **LISTEN, FIND AND POINT.**

6 LISTEN AND STICK.

7 LOOK, THINK AND MATCH.

8 LOOK, LISTEN AND SAY.

WHAT'S THIS?

IT'S A BIKE.

9 LOOK, POINT AND TALK.

10 PRESS OUT AND PLAY.

11 LISTEN, NUMBER AND SING!

WHAT'S YOUR FAVORITE TOY?

1 WHAT'S YOUR FAVORITE TOY?
CAN YOU GUESS? CAN YOU GUESS?
I THINK IT'S A BALL.
OH YES, OH YES!

2 WHAT'S YOUR FAVORITE TOY?
CAN YOU GUESS? CAN YOU GUESS?
I THINK IT'S A KITE.
OH YES, OH YES!

3 WHAT'S YOUR FAVORITE TOY?
CAN YOU GUESS? CAN YOU GUESS?
I THINK IT'S AN ART SET.
OH YES, OH YES!

4 WHAT'S YOUR FAVORITE TOY?
CAN YOU GUESS? CAN YOU GUESS?
I THINK IT'S A BIKE.
OH YES, OH YES!

I HAVE AN IDEA.
CAN YOU GUESS? CAN YOU GUESS?
WANNA PLAY TOGETHER?
OH YES, OH YES!

UNIT 5

12 DO THE CROSSWORD PUZZLE.

13 LOOK, LISTEN AND SAY.

14 DRAW AND TALK.

HERE AND NOW

COOPERATION

1 THINK AND CHECK.

2 LOOK AND THINK. THEN DRAW AND TALK.

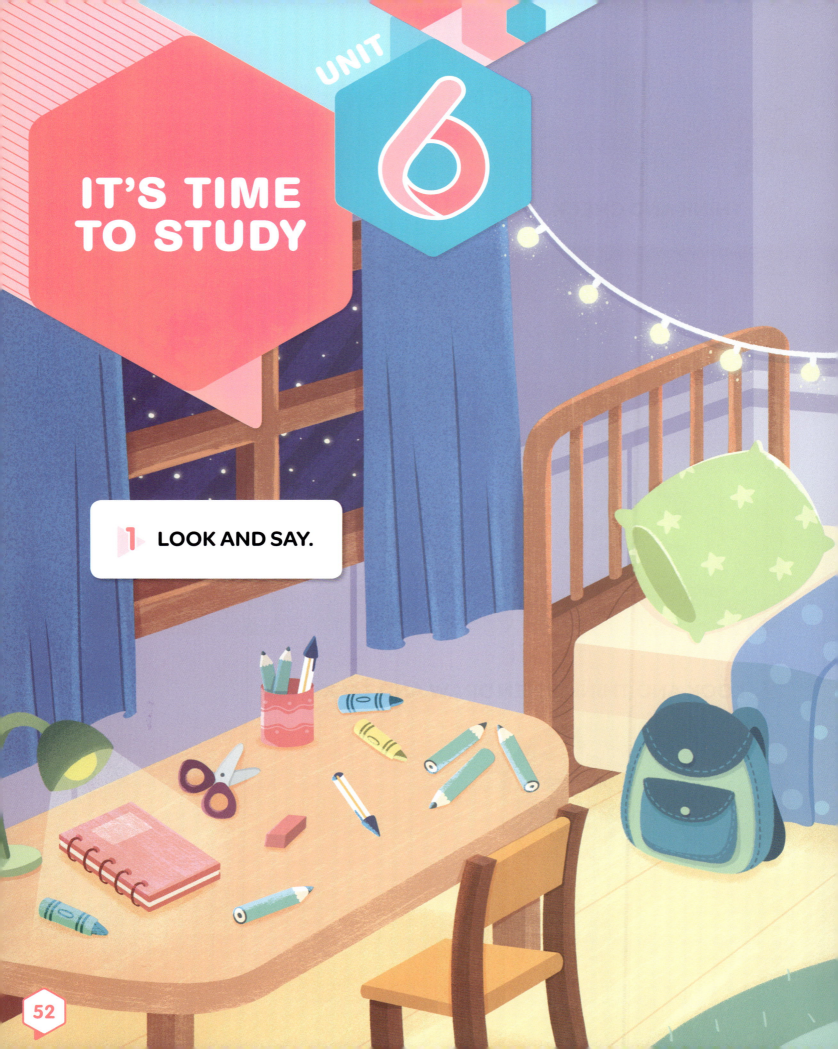

3 LOOK, LISTEN AND SAY.

1. A BACKPACK
2. A BOOK
3. A CRAYON
4. AN ERASER
5. A NOTEBOOK
6. A PEN
7. A PENCIL

4 LOOK, FIND AND CIRCLE.

5 LISTEN, LOOK AND CHECK.

6 LOOK, THINK AND DRAW.

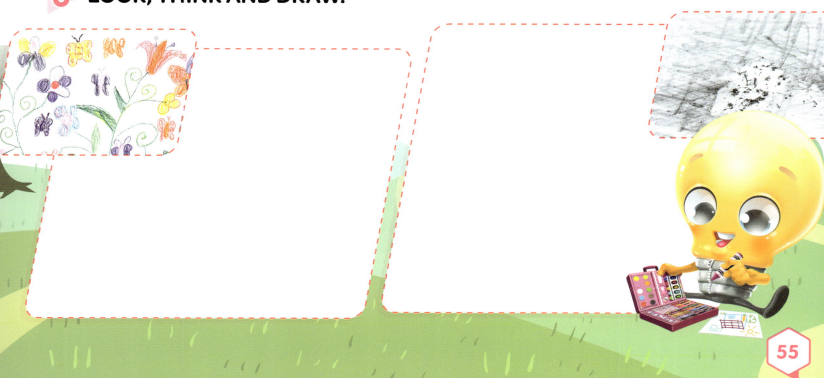

55

7 LOOK, LISTEN AND SAY.

8 TALK AND STICK.

Learn more!
http://mod.lk/fai1_u6

9 PRESS OUT AND PLAY.

10 LISTEN, DRAW AND SING.

ALWAYS BE GENTLE

GENTLE, GENTLE, ALWAYS BE GENTLE.
GENTLE, GENTLE, ALWAYS BE GENTLE.

OH, PLEASE!
I NEED AN ERASER, A BOOK AND A PENCIL.
HERE YOU ARE.
OH, THANK YOU!
THANK YOU! THANK YOU! THANK YOU!

GENTLE, GENTLE, ALWAYS BE GENTLE.
GENTLE, GENTLE, ALWAYS BE GENTLE.

OH, PLEASE!
I NEED A NOTEBOOK, A CRAYON AND A PEN.
HERE YOU ARE.
OH, THANK YOU!
THANK YOU! THANK YOU! THANK YOU!

GENTLE, GENTLE, ALWAYS BE GENTLE.
GENTLE, GENTLE, ALWAYS BE GENTLE.
ALWAYS BE GENTLE.

11 FIND THE 7 DIFFERENCES.

12 PLAY AND GUESS!

I NEED AN ERASER.

HERE YOU ARE.

OOPS, IT'S A BOOK!

58

CLIL SCHOOL OBJECTS (SCIENCE)

1 LOOK, LISTEN AND NUMBER. THEN DISCUSS.

A

B

2 LOOK, THINK AND MATCH.

3 THINK AND DRAW.

59

REVIEW 5 & 6

1. LISTEN AND NUMBER.

2. COLOR BY CODE.

3 LISTEN AND CIRCLE. THEN COUNT AND WRITE.

3 LOOK, LISTEN AND SAY.

1 BATHROOM

2 BEDROOM

3 DINING ROOM

4 KITCHEN

5 LIVING ROOM

6 YARD

4 LISTEN, FIND AND CIRCLE.

5 DRAW.

6 LOOK, LISTEN AND SAY. THEN MATCH.

1.  CIRCLE
2.  RECTANGLE
3.  SQUARE
4.  TRIANGLE

 A
 B
 C
 D

7 LOOK, LISTEN AND NUMBER.

 A
 B
 C
 D
 E
 F

8 LOOK, LISTEN AND SAY.

9 STICK AND TALK.

10 PRESS OUT AND PLAY.

11 LISTEN, DRAW AND SING.

WHERE'S THE CIRCLE?

WHERE'S THE CIRCLE?
LOOK, THE WINDOW IS A CIRCLE!

WHERE'S THE WINDOW?
IN THE LIVING ROOM.

WHERE'S THE LIVING ROOM?
IN THE HOUSE.

WHERE'S THE HOUSE?
IN THE STREET.

WHERE'S THE STREET?
IN THE CITY.

WHERE'S THE CITY?
IN THE COUNTRY.

WHERE'S THE COUNTRY?
IN THE WORLD.

LOOK, THE WORLD
IS A CIRCLE TOO!

12 LOOK AND CHECK.

☐ A CIRCLE ☐ A SQUARE   ☐ A RECTANGLE ☐ A TRIANGLE

☐ A TRIANGLE ☐ A SQUARE   ☐ A RECTANGLE ☐ A CIRCLE

13 CREATE WITH SHAPES. THEN TALK.

HERE AND NOW

USING MINDFULNESS TO ORGANIZE

1 **LISTEN, FIND AND CIRCLE.**

2 **THINK AND CHECK. THEN DISCUSS.**

1.

2.

69

3 LOOK, LISTEN AND SAY.

1. APPLES
2. BANANAS
3. CAKE
4. COOKIES
5. MILK
6. ORANGE JUICE
7. TOAST

Learn more!
http://mod.lk/fai1_u8

4 LOOK, LISTEN AND SAY. THEN DRAW AND COLOR.

I DON'T LIKE

I LIKE

I LOVE

5 LISTEN, FIND AND POINT.

72

6 LOOK, LISTEN AND NUMBER.

7 WHAT'S MISSING? LOOK AND STICK.

1. APPLE
2. BANANAS
3. CAKE
4. COOKIES
5. MILK
6. ORANGE JUICE
7. TOAST

8 **LOOK, LISTEN AND SAY.**

9 **DRAW AND TALK.**

10 **PRESS OUT AND PLAY.**

11 LISTEN, POINT AND SING.

OH, I'M HUNGRY,
I'M VERY, VERY HUNGRY!
PLEASE HAVE A COOKIE.
YUMMY! COOKIES!

OH, I'M HUNGRY,
I'M STILL VERY HUNGRY!
PLEASE HAVE AN APPLE.
YUMMY! COOKIES AND APPLES!

OH, I'M HUNGRY,
I'M STILL VERY HUNGRY!
PLEASE HAVE SOME TOAST.
YUMMY! COOKIES, APPLES
AND TOAST!

OH, I'M HUNGRY,
I'M STILL VERY HUNGRY!
PLEASE HAVE SOME CAKE.
YUMMY! COOKIES, APPLES,
TOAST AND CAKE!

OH, I'M HUNGRY,
I'M STILL VERY HUNGRY!
PLEASE HAVE A BANANA.
YUMMY! COOKIES, APPLES,
TOAST, CAKE AND BANANAS!
NOW I'M REALLY FULL!

12 GUESS WHO? LOOK AND PLAY.

FOOD AND CLOTHES (GEOGRAPHY)

1 ► LOOK AND MATCH.

2 ► THINK AND COLOR.

 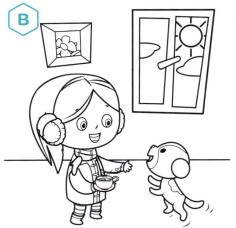 

REVIEW 7 & 8

1 IDENTIFY AND NUMBER.

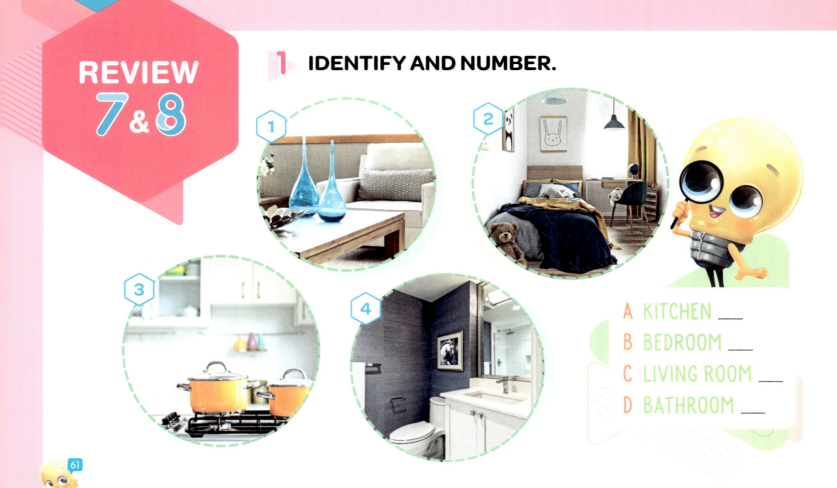

A KITCHEN ___
B BEDROOM ___
C LIVING ROOM ___
D BATHROOM ___

2 LISTEN AND COLOR.

3 THINK AND STICK. THEN LOOK, READ AND DRAW.

1. I 😊 BANANAS.
2. I 😊 ORANGE JUICE AND MILK.

3. I 😊 COOKIES AND APPLES.

4. I 😊 CAKE AND TOAST.

HANDS ON

MAKING A POSTER OF OUR PETS

1 MIME YOUR PET.

2 LOOK AND ORDER.

3 LOOK AND WRITE *B*, *A* OR *S*.

4 MAKE A POSTER.

MAKING A ZOOM BALL

▶ **1** TALK ABOUT TOYS.

▶ **2** LOOK AND SAY. THEN CHECK.

1 BOARD GAME

2 CARDBOARD TOY

3 GALIMOTO

4 PIÑATA

5 RUBIK'S CUBE

6 ZOOM BALL

▶ **3** MAKE A ZOOM BALL.

INSTRUCTIONS

CHECK

CIRCLE

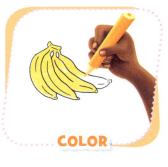
COLOR

Learn more!
http://mod.lk/class1

COUNT

DANCE

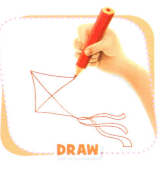
DRAW

FIND

LISTEN

LOOK

MATCH

NUMBER

PLAY

POINT

PRESS OUT

SAY

SING

STICK

TALK

THINK

WRITE

GLOSSARY

UNIT 1

BABY: BEBÊ
BIG: GRANDE
BROTHER: IRMÃO
CHILDREN: CRIANÇAS

DAD: PAPAI
ELDERLY: IDOSOS
FAMILY: FAMÍLIA
GRANDMA: VOVÓ
GRANDPA: VOVÔ
I LOVE MY FAMILY!: EU AMO MINHA FAMÍLIA!
IT DOESN'T MATTER: NÃO IMPORTA
JUST: APENAS
LOVE: AMAR
MOM: MAMÃE
PHOTO ALBUM: ÁLBUM DE FOTOS
POPSICLE: PICOLÉ

RESPECT: RESPEITAR; RESPEITO
SISTER: IRMÃ
SMALL: PEQUENO(A)
THEM ALL: TODOS ELES
THIS: ESTE/ESTA
TIC-TAC-TOE: JOGO DA VELHA

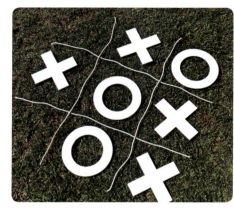

UNIT 2

ART: ARTE
BALL PIT: PISCINA DE BOLINHAS

BLACK: PRETO(A)
BLUE: AZUL
BROWN: MARROM
CAN: PODER (VERBO)
CODE: CÓDIGO
COLORS: CORES
CONTRASTING: CONTRASTANTE(S)
COUPLE: CASAL
DONUT: ROSQUINHA (DOCE)

FAVORITE: FAVORITO(A)
FUN: DIVERSÃO
GRAY: CINZA
GREEN: VERDE
JUNGLE GYM: TREPA-TREPA
MAKE: FAZER
ODD ONE OUT: QUE NÃO PERTENCE
ORANGE: LARANJA
PINK: COR-DE-ROSA
PLAY: BRINCAR
PLAYGROUND: PARQUE INFANTIL
PURPLE: ROXO(A)
RED: VERMELHO(A)
RIDING: ANDAR A CAVALO, CAVALGAR
SEESAW: GANGORRA
SLIDE: ESCORREGADOR
SOUNDS: SONS
SWING: BALANÇO
TRAMPOLINE: PULA-PULA
WHITE: BRANCO(A)
YELLOW: AMARELO(A)

UNIT 3

ADOPT: ADOTAR
ALL ABOUT: TUDO SOBRE

85

CAT: GATO
CHUBBY: GORDINHO(A)

CUTE: FOFO(A)
DICTATION: DITADO
DOG: CACHORRO
FERRET: FURÃO
HAMSTER: *HAMSTER*
HAS: TEM
HOW MANY: QUANTOS(AS)
LITTLE: PEQUENO(S), PEQUENA(S)
MINDFULNESS: ATENÇÃO PLENA
PETS: ANIMAIS DE ESTIMAÇÃO
PICTURE: IMAGEM
RABBIT: COELHO
TURTLE: TARTARUGA
WHAT'S THIS?: O QUE É ISSO?

ARMS: BRAÇOS
BODY: CORPO
CHOREOGRAPHY: COREOGRAFIA
CLAP: BATER (PALMAS)
DANCE: DANÇAR
EARS: ORELHAS
EYES: OLHOS

FEET: PÉS
HAIR: CABELO
HANDS: MÃOS
HAVE: TER
HEAD: CABEÇA
HEADPHONE: FONE DE OUVIDO
HULA-HOOP: BAMBOLÊ

HUMAN BODY: CORPO HUMANO
LEGS: PERNAS
LIKE: GOSTAR; DA MESMA FORMA QUE
MOUTH: BOCA
MOVE: MOVER, MEXER
NOSE: NARIZ
ROBOT: ROBÔ
ROPE: CORDA
SCIENCE: CIÊNCIAS
STAMP: BATER (OS PÉS)
TEETH: DENTES

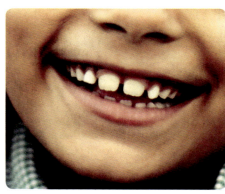

THIS IS MY BODY: ESTE É MEU CORPO
TONGUE: LÍNGUA
TOUCH: TOCAR
WASH: LAVAR

ART SET: ESTOJO DE ARTES
BALL: BOLA
BIKE: BICICLETA
BRUSH: PINCEL
BUILDING BLOCKS: BLOCOS DE MONTAR

CAN: CONSEGUIR
CAR: CARRO
COOPERATION: COOPERAÇÃO
CROSSWORD PUZZLE: PALAVRAS-
  -CRUZADAS

DOLL: BONECA
GUESS: ADIVINHAR
KITE: PIPA
LET'S...: VAMOS...
MARKER: CANETINHA COLORIDA
MISSING: FALTANDO

GLOSSARY

ORGANIZE: ORGANIZAR
PAINT: TINTA
SCISSORS: TESOURA
TEDDY BEAR: URSO DE PELÚCIA
TOYS: BRINQUEDOS

WANNA (WANT TO): QUER

ALWAYS: SEMPRE
BACKPACK: MOCHILA

BOOK: LIVRO
CRAYON: GIZ DE CERA
DIFFERENCES: DIFERENÇAS
ERASER: BORRACHA
GENTLE: GENTIL
HERE YOU ARE: AQUI ESTÁ/ESTÃO
LOCKER: ARMÁRIO (ESCOLAR)

NEED: PRECISAR
NOTEBOOK: CADERNO
PEN: CANETA
PENCIL: LÁPIS
PENCIL CASE: ESTOJO
PLEASE: POR FAVOR
RULERS: RÉGUAS
SCHOOL OBJECTS: MATERIAIS ESCOLARES
SOME: ALGUNS/ALGUMAS; UM POUCO DE
STUDY: ESTUDAR
THANK YOU!: OBRIGADO(A)!
TIME: HORA
TRASH: LIXO

BATHROOM: BANHEIRO
BEDROOM: QUARTO
CIRCLE: CÍRCULO
CITY: CIDADE

COUNTRY: PAÍS
CREATE: CRIAR
DINING ROOM: SALA DE JANTAR
FIND THE WAY: ENCONTRE O CAMINHO
HOME: LAR
KITCHEN: COZINHA
LIVING ROOM: SALA DE ESTAR
LOOK: OLHAR
RECTANGLE: RETÂNGULO
ROOF: TELHADO
SHAPES: FORMAS
SQUARE: QUADRADO
STREET: RUA

87

TRIANGLE: TRIÂNGULO
TOO: TAMBÉM
USING: USANDO
WALL: PAREDE
WHERE: ONDE
WINDOW: JANELA
YARD: QUINTAL

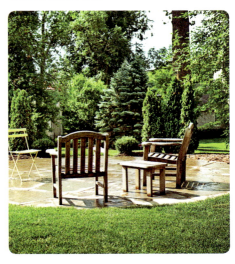

APPLES: MAÇÃS
BANANAS: BANANAS
BASKET: CESTA
BIKINI: BIQUÍNI
CAKE: BOLO

CLOTHES: ROUPAS
CLOUDY DAY: DIA NUBLADO

COOKIES: BISCOITOS
DON'T LIKE: NÃO GOSTAR
FOOD: ALIMENTOS, COMIDAS
FULL: SATISFEITO(A)

GEOGRAPHY: GEOGRAFIA
GUESS WHO?: ADIVINHA QUEM É?
HOT CHOCOLATE: CHOCOLATE QUENTE
HUNGRY: COM FOME
LIKE: GOSTAR
MILK: LEITE
ORANGE JUICE: SUCO DE LARANJA
PICNIC: PIQUENIQUE
REALLY: REALMENTE
SHORTS: SHORTS
SNACK: LANCHE
SOUP: SOPA
STILL: AINDA
SUNNY DAY: DIA ENSOLARADO

T-SHIRT: CAMISETA
TOAST: TORRADA
VERY: MUITO
WATERMELON: MELANCIA

NAME: _____ CLASS: _____

WORKBOOK
UNIT 1

1 **LOOK AND STICK.**

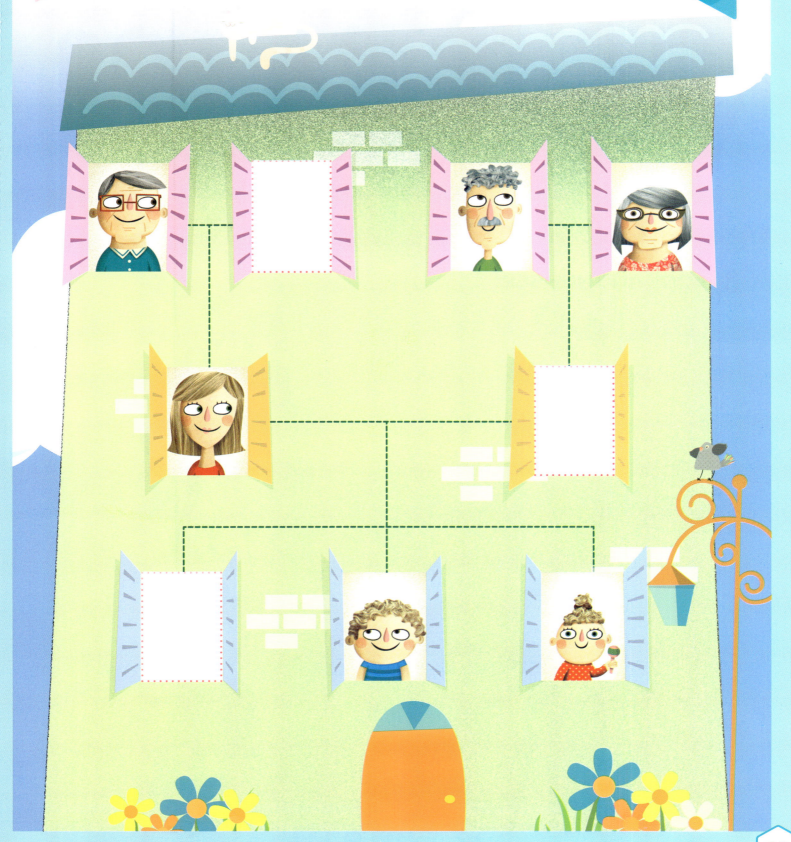

89

2 LOOK AND CIRCLE.

3 LOOK AND NUMBER.

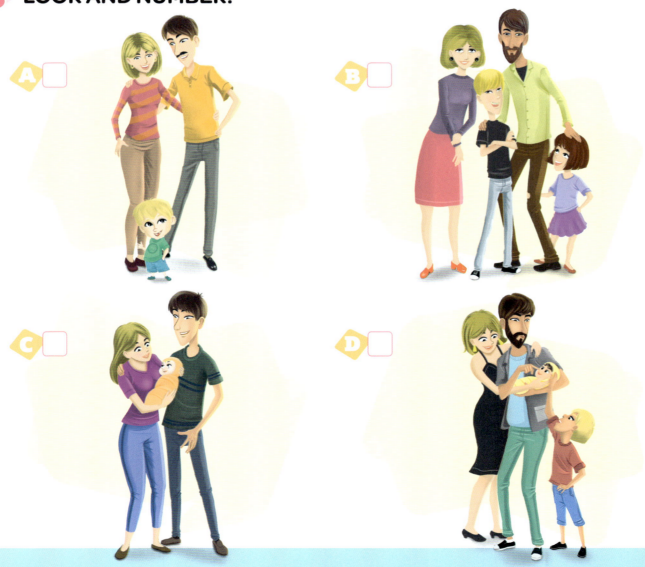

NAME: _____   CLASS: _____

1 COLOR BY CODE TO FIND THE PLAYGROUND.

91

2 CIRCLE THE ODD ONE OUT.

3 LOOK AND CHECK.

1. ☐ BLUE ☐ GRAY
2. ☐ PURPLE ☐ ORANGE
3. ☐ RED ☐ YELLOW
4. ☐ GREEN ☐ PINK

NAME: _____   CLASS: _____

WORKBOOK
UNIT 3

1   LOOK AND COLOR.

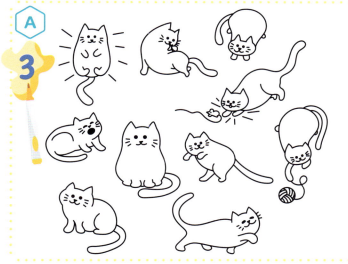
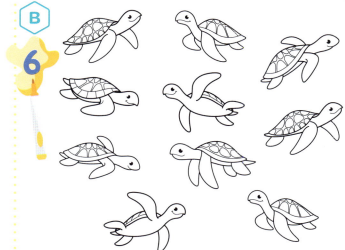

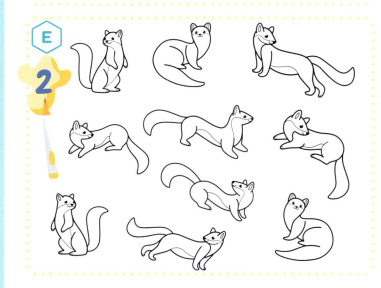

93

2 LOOK AND NUMBER.

3 FIND THE 6 DIFFERENCES.

NAME: _____ CLASS: _____

1 LOOK, COUNT AND WRITE.

95

2 LOOK, THINK AND CHECK.

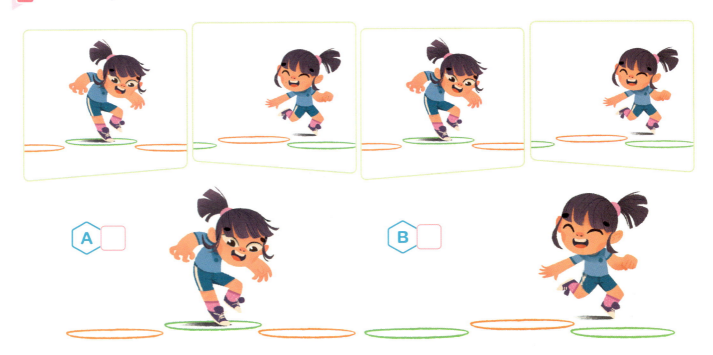

3 LOOK AND MATCH.

NAME: _____ CLASS: _____

1 LOOK, FIND AND CIRCLE. THEN DRAW.

97

2 LOOK AND NUMBER. THEN COLOR.

3 CIRCLE THE ODD ONE OUT.

98

NAME: _____   CLASS: _____

WORKBOOK
UNIT 6

1 LOOK, COUNT AND COMPLETE.

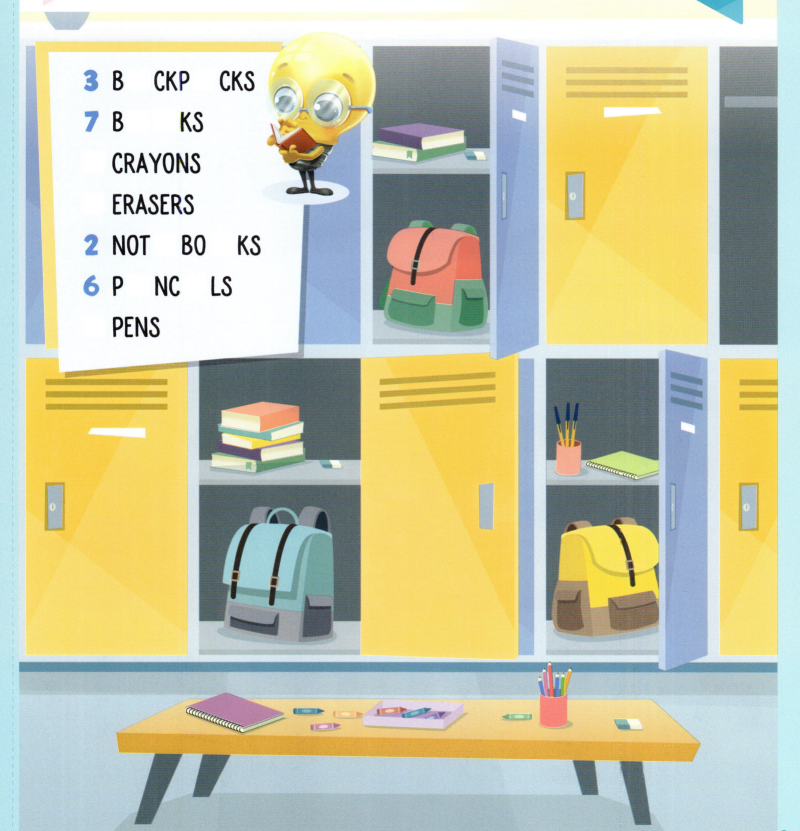

3 B CKP CKS
7 B   KS
  CRAYONS
  ERASERS
2 NOT BO KS
6 P NC LS
  PENS

99

2 LOOK AND NUMBER.

3 LOOK, READ AND CIRCLE.

WORKBOOK

UNIT 7

NAME: _____ CLASS: _____

1 FIND THE WAY TO THE SHAPES.

1

2

3

4

A

B

C

D

101

2 LOOK AND COUNT. THEN COLOR.

3 LOOK, UNSCRAMBLE AND WRITE.

INGDIN OROM

ARDY

DEBRMOO

IVILNG RMOO

KCIHTEN

OROMBTAH

WORKBOOK

UNIT 8

NAME: _____   CLASS: _____

1 CONNECT THE DOTS. THEN COLOR AND NUMBER.

A ☐ COOKIES

B ☐ BANANAS

C ☐ MILK

D ☐ APPLES

E ☐ CAKE

F ☐ TOAST

G ☐ ORANGE JUICE

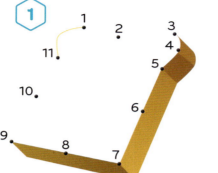
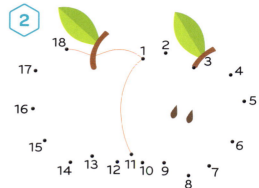
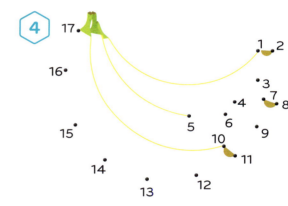
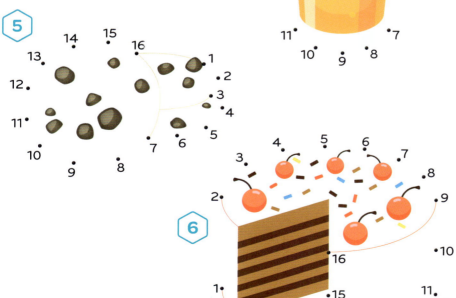
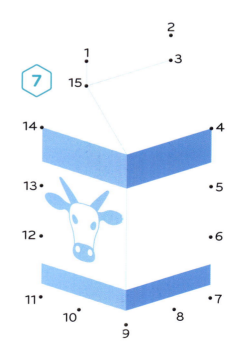

103

2 LOOK AND NUMBER.

3 LOOK AND COMPLETE.

I LIKE _____, _____ AND _____.
I DON'T LIKE _____, _____ AND _____.

FOLD

GLUE

105

107

UNIT 3

UNIT 4

 FOLD

UNIT 5

ART SET

BIKE

DOLL

TEDDY BEAR

BALL

CAR

KITE

PRESS-OUTS

UNIT 6

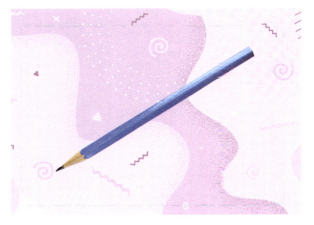

115

UNIT 7

117

UNIT 8

PRESS-OUTS

119

UNIT 1

UNIT 2

REVIEW 1 & 2

UNIT 3

UNIT

REVIEW 3 & 4

UNIT 5

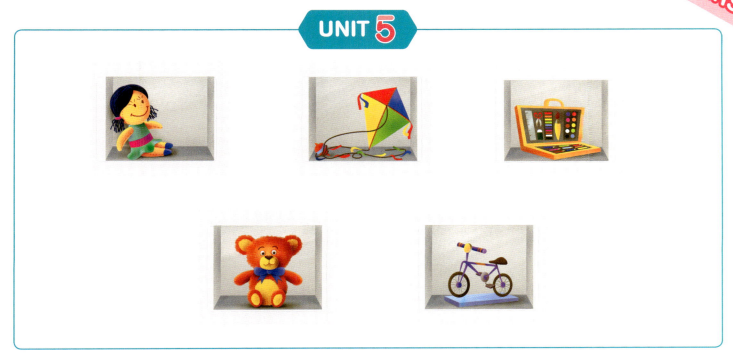

UNIT 6

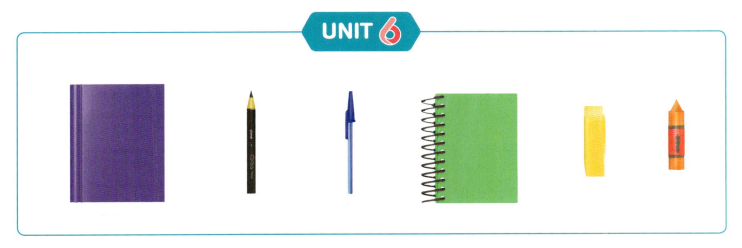

UNIT 7

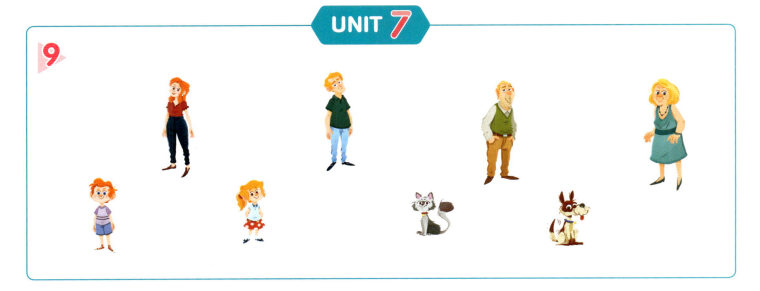

STICKERS

UNIT 7

13

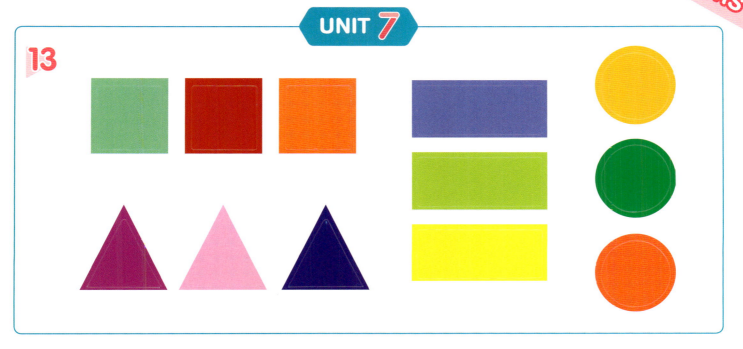

UNIT 8

REVIEW 7 & 8

127

HANDS ON

WORKBOOK UNIT 1

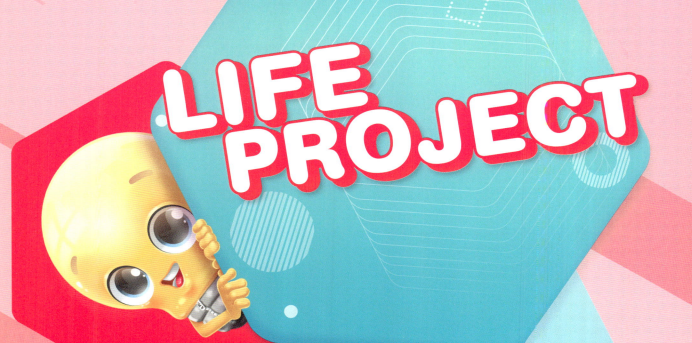

Direção editorial: Sandra Possas

Edição executiva de inglês: Izaura Valverde
Edição executiva de produção e multimídia: Adriana Pedro de Almeida

Coordenação de arte e produção: Raquel Buim
Coordenação de revisão: Rafael Spigel

Edição de texto: Nathália Horvath
Elaboração de conteúdo: Nathália Horvath, Sílvia Beraldo
Preparação de originais: Helaine Albuquerque
Revisão: Carolina Waideman, Flora Vaz Manzione, Kandy Saraiva, Lucila Vrublevicius Segóvia, Márcio Martins, Vivian Cristina de Souza

Projeto gráfico: Elaine Alves, Karina de Sá
Edição de arte: Elaine Alves
Diagramação: Casa de Ideias
Capa: Karina de Sá, Raquel Buim
Ilustração de capa: Leo Teixeira
Ilustrações: Bianca Aguiar, Kézia Trentini, Leo Teixeira, Maria Lúcia Rigon, Raíssa Bulhões
Artes: Elaine Alves

Iconografia: Danielle de Alcântara, Paloma Klein, Sara Alencar
Coordenação de *bureau*: Rubens M. Rodrigues
Tratamento de imagens: Ademir Francisco Baptista, Joel Aparecido, Luiz Carlos Costa, Marina M. Buzzinaro, Vânia Aparecida M. de Oliveira
Pré-impressão: Alexandre Petreca, Everton L. de Oliveira, Fabio Roldan, Marcio H. Kamoto, Ricardo Rodrigues, Vitória Sousa
Áudio: Núcleo de Criação Produções em Áudio
Impressão e acabamento: HRosa Gráfica e Editora
Lote: 797804
Cod: 51120002130

Créditos das fotos: p. 4: ©NYC Health, ©daboost/Istockphoto, ©Martin Holverda/Istockphoto; p. 5: ©michaeljung/Istockphoto, ©czarny_bez/Istockphoto, ©Khosrork/Istockphoto; p. 7: ©KanKhem/Istockphoto, ©Victor_Brave/Istockphoto, ©Lisitsa/Istockphoto, ©Imgorthand/Istockphoto, ©jamesjoong/Istockphoto, ©Oleksandr Pupko/Istockphoto, ©guru86/Istockphoto; p. 8: ©evgenyatamanenko/Istockphoto, ©PeopleImages/Istockphoto, ©HRAUN/Istockphoto, ©FatCamera/Istockphoto, ©popcorner/Shutterstock, ©kali9/Istockphoto, ©max-kegfire/Istockphoto, ©max-kegfire/Istockphoto, ©Lacheev/Istockphoto, ©skynesher/Istockphoto, ©monkeybusinessimages/Istockphoto; p. 9: ©monkeybusinessimages/Istockphoto, ©tbd/Istockphoto, ©monkeybusinessimages/Istockphoto, ©monkeybusinessimages/Istockphoto, ©monkeybusinessimages/Istockphoto, ©monkeybusinessimages/Istockphoto, ©Thais Ceneviva/Istockphoto, ©Wavebreakmedia/Istockphoto, ©brittak/Istockphoto, ©czarny_bez/Istockphoto, ©czarny_bez/Istockphoto, ©DragonImages/Istockphoto; p. 11: ©Inna Tolstorebrova/Istockphoto, ©Nungning20/Istockphoto; p. 12: ©pinstock/Istockphoto, ©fotokostic/Istockphoto, ©alvarez/Istockphoto, ©Lapina/Shutterstock, ©HRAUN/Istockphoto, ©gpointstudio/Istockphoto, ©Dusan Stankovic/Istockphoto, ©MoMorad/Istockphoto; p. 13: ©Seubsai/Istockphoto, ©CreativaImages/Istockphoto, ©FG Trade/Istockphoto, ©Tomwang112/Istockphoto, ©selimaksan/Istockphoto, ©oshcherban/Istockphoto; p. 14: ©damedeeso/Istockphoto, ©diignat/Istockphoto, ©Moyo Studio/Istockphoto, ©somdul/Istockphoto; p. 15: ©Corbis/Getty Images, ©bymuratdeniz/Istockphoto, ©Leylaynr/Istockphoto, ©miljko/Istockphoto, ©czarny_bez/Istockphoto; p. 16: ©monzenmachi/Istockphoto, ©Wavebreakmedia/Istockphoto, ©Natee127/Istockphoto, ©PeopleImages/Istockphoto; p. 17: ©eggeeggjiew/Istockphoto, ©fizkes/Istockphoto, ©yulkapopkova/Istockphoto; p. 18: ©Dobrila Vignjevic/Istockphoto, ©MamikaStock/Istockphoto, ©BrianAJackson/Istockphoto, ©Arsenii Palivoda/Istockphoto, ©da-kuk/Istockphoto, twomeows/Getty Images, ©Hispanolistic/Istockphoto, ©Bigandt_Photography/Istockphoto; p. 19: ©FatCamera/Istockphoto, ©czarny_bez/Istockphoto, ©Ruta Lipskija/Istockphoto, ©kurmungadd/Istockphoto, ©happyfoto/Istockphoto, ©malerapaso/Istockphoto, ©Elenakirey/Istockphoto.

Todos os *sites* mencionados nesta obra foram reproduzidos apenas para fins didáticos. A Richmond não tem controle sobre seu conteúdo, o qual foi cuidadosamente verificado antes de sua utilização.
Websites mentioned in this material were quoted for didactic purposes only. Richmond has no control over their content and urges care when using them.

Embora todas as medidas tenham sido tomadas para identificar e contatar os detentores de direitos autorais sobre os materiais reproduzidos nesta obra, isso nem sempre foi possível.
A editora estará pronta a retificar quaisquer erros dessa natureza assim que notificada.
Every effort has been made to trace the copyright holders, but if any omission can be rectified, the publishers will be pleased to make the necessary arrangements.

Reprodução proibida. Art. 184 do Código Penal e Lei 9.610 de 19 de fevereiro de 1998.

Todos os direitos reservados.

RICHMOND
SANTILLANA EDUCAÇÃO LTDA.
Rua Padre Adelino, 758, 3º andar – Belenzinho
São Paulo – SP – Brasil – CEP 03303-904
www.richmond.com.br
2024
Impresso no Brasil

CONTENTS

MY ORIGIN 4

CHILDREN HAVE VALUES 6

MY DREAMS 8

KEEP TRYING! 10

I CAN DO IT! 12

OUR RESPONSIBILITIES 14

THIS IS SO DIFFICULT! 16

LET'S BREATH! 18

MY ORIGIN

1 LOOK, LISTEN AND CHECK.

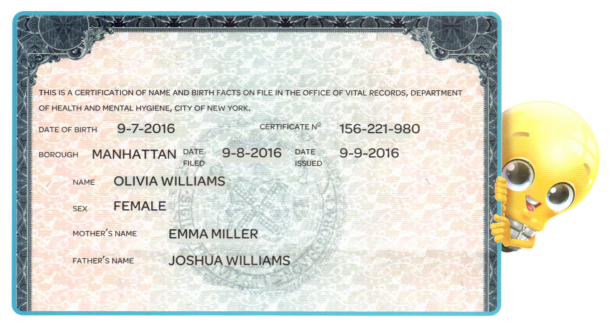

1 ☐ MOM'S AND DAD'S NAMES.
2 ☐ SISTERS' AND BROTHERS' NAMES.
3 ☐ GRANDMA'S AND GRANDPA'S NAMES.
4 ☐ BIRTHDAY.

MOM = MOTHER
DAD = FATHER

2 COMPARE, THINK AND MATCH.

FAMILY TIME!

3 MAKE A BOOKLET ABOUT YOUR ORIGIN.

STEP 1 — CHOOSE PHOTOS TO TELL YOUR FAMILY HISTORY.

STEP 2 — FIND OUT INFORMATION ABOUT YOUR FAMILY.

STEP 3 — USE PAPER OR A COMPUTER.

STEP 4 — GLUE THE PHOTOS AND WRITE CAPTIONS. ASK YOUR FAMILY TO HELP YOU.

STEP 5 — ADD MORE INFORMATION.

STEP 6 — DECORATE YOUR BOOKLET.

4 LET'S DRAW AND GUESS THE FAMILY MEMBER!

THIS IS THE GRANDPA!

CHILDREN HAVE VALUES

1 LOOK, THINK AND CIRCLE.

2 THINK AND DRAW.

FAMILY TIME!

3 LET'S PLAY A BOARD GAME!

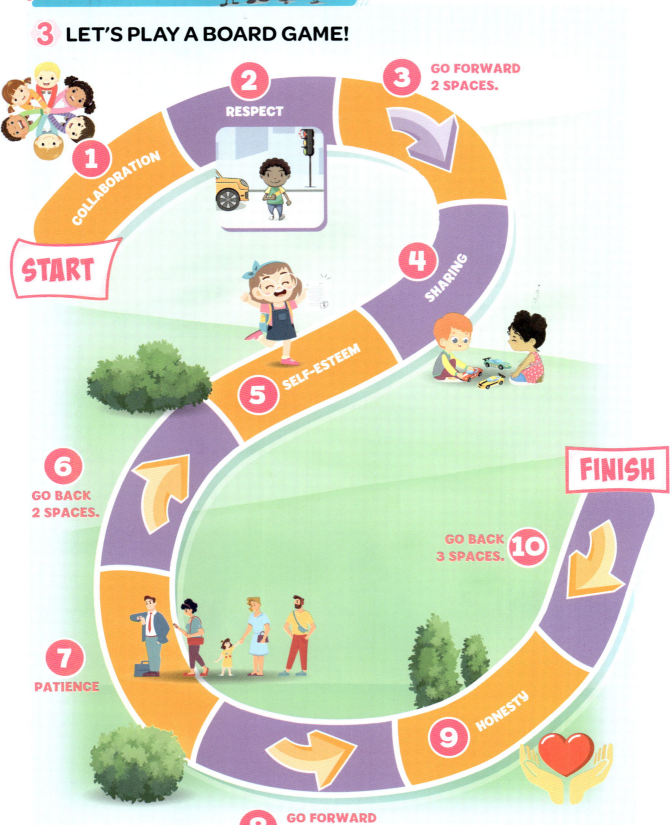

MY DREAMS

1 LOOK AND TALK.

2 LOOK AND MATCH.

3 LOOK AND TALK.

4 DRAW AND SHARE.

FAMILY TIME!

5 LET'S MAKE COLLAGES!

KEEP TRYING!

1 LOOK AND TALK.

2 LOOK AND NUMBER.

3 SHOW AND TELL.

FAMILY TIME!

4 LET'S CREATE A FAMILY GARDEN!

5 GROUP CHALLENGE.

I CAN DO IT!

1 LOOK AND TALK.

2 LOOK AND MATCH.

3 LOOK, CIRCLE AND DRAW.

FAMILY TIME!

4 ACTION!

5 LET'S CREATE!

OUR RESPONSIBILITIES

1 LOOK AND CHOOSE.

2 LOOK AND COLOR.

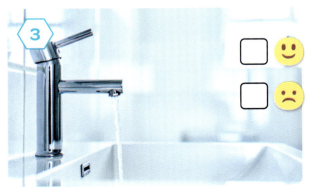

3 LOOK AND CHECK.

FAMILY TIME!

4 MAKE A RESPONSIBILITY CHART.

NAME	RESPONSIBILITY	MON	TUE	WED	THU	FRI	SAT	SUN

5 GROUP WORK.

THIS IS SO DIFFICULT!

1 LOOK AND TALK.

2 LOOK AND CIRCLE.

3 **LET'S PLAY BINGO!**

4 **LET'S PRACTICE!**

 FOLLOW INSTRUCTIONS
 STAY FOCUSED
 BE ORGANIZED

LET'S BREATH!

1 LOOK AND CIRCLE.

2 LOOK, THINK AND CHECK.

3 LET'S MEDITATE!

4 THINK AND DRAW.

FAMILY TIME!

5 MAKE YOUR STRESS BALL!

STEP 1 YOU NEED FLOUR, A FUNNEL, BALLOONS AND MARKERS.

STEP 2 USE THE FUNNEL TO PUT THE FLOUR INTO THE BALLOONS.

STEP 3 USE THE MARKERS TO DRAW FACES ON THE BALLOONS.